Something Stayed.

Vishwam Bagrodia

BookLeaf
Publishing

India | USA | UK

Made with ❤ on the BookLeaf Publishing Platform
www.bookleafpub.in
www.bookleafpub.com

Dedication

For Mom and Dad
whose quiet strength and boundless love gave me the
courage to feel deeply and speak softly.

Preface

I never meant to write this. Well, at least not like this. These poems weren't planned. They weren't sculpted. They just... arrived. Uninvited, like memories do, well some. The kind that linger long after the moment has passed. The kind that you can hear beneath your skin when the world gets quiet enough. I thought I'd left certain things behind. Places. People. Versions of myself I outgrew or perhaps pretended to. But they didn't leave. They curled up in the corners of me, waiting in silence, and one day, they began to speak.

This book is what they said. **"Something Stayed."** That's what I've come to understand. No matter how far you run, how much you let go, how brave you pretend to be; something always stays. A voice. A scent. A sentence you didn't say. A city that never really forgave you. A face that keeps showing up in other people. A version of you that looks back through glass. And maybe... maybe what stays isn't always meant to. Maybe it isn't beautiful, or fair, or wanted. But it's honest. And sometimes, it's all we have. These poems are my way of holding onto that, the ache that didn't ask permission. The tenderness that outlived the love. The ghosts that kept showing up long after I stopped calling their names.

They're fragments of what I couldn't bury. Proof that I felt something, even if I couldn't make sense of it at the time. Even if it was just a flicker in a storm.

So if you're here,
if you're holding this book and wondering
why your chest tightens when you turn the page—
maybe something stayed with you, too.
And maybe, just maybe,
that means we're not alone in it.
Thank you for carrying this with me.
For listening to the things I never said out loud.
This is my heart,
laid bare in verse.
Not to be fixed—
just to be heard.

~With everything that stayed,

Vishwam Bagrodia

Acknowledgements

"We are, each of us, a chorus of those who have loved us."
~ Rupi Kaur

This book would not exist without the quiet strength and unconditional love of my parents. Thank you, Dad and Mom, for being the ground beneath my every step and the calm in my every storm.
To my dearest friends - Kavan, Harsh, Aakansha, Vinayak and Akansha - your unwavering support, constant encouragement, and belief in my voice have carried me through every doubt and silence. I'm very grateful for your presence on this journey, and in my life.
To my grandfather, whose support steadies and grounds me; to my sister, whose presence is a refuge; to my Jiju, whose quiet faith in me has never wavered, and my family, thank you for believing not just in my words, but in who I am becoming.
You've all been the steady hands behind these pages.
This is as much yours as it is mine.

Hiraeth

Beneath the sky, a muted grey,
I wander where the winds once sang.
The path I knew, now lost, decayed,
As whispers fade, the echoes hang.

The walls once warm, now cracked and cold,
A hearth that flickered, now erased,
I search for roots, but find no hold,
Just empty space where love was placed.

The fields I tilled now wear a veil
Of dust and sorrow, choked and dry.
Each step I take, my soul grows frail,
A fleeting hope, a silent cry.

In hollowed dreams, I ache and bleed,
A yearning buried deep within,
For lands I'll never touch again
A home that's lost, a life forsaken.

The winds are harsh, the light is dim,
The shadows mock the tears I weep.
In endless longing, I begin
To fade, while memories fall asleep.

The Cenotaph

The Streets are dark in broad daylight
With poles now moving around
A tryst oh now with despair and me
While I move down aground.

The smell of soot did I bear well
On costs of life and creed
The mud and boot did I wear with pride
Have I done well indeed?

The drear and dearth and filth around
And yet new walls being built
And tears there give food to many
Shackles for those without guilt.

Oh how they whet their daggers there
On costs of life and creed
The last morning sun with my third eye I see
Have I done well indeed?

Have...I done well indeed?

Wraith

The air is thick with blood and ash,
As shadows twist and grind the sky,
Each step I take, the ground will crash,
Beneath the weight of all I've tried.

The distant cries, they fill the air,
But none are mine—yet still, they call,
I see the faces, feel the stare,
Of those who fought, then fell, then crawled.

My hands are stained, my mind is torn,
Between the need to fight or flee,
A ghost of me, a man reborn,
Yet lost in this unholy sea.

The echo of my heartbeat fades,
Drowned by screams I cannot quell,
In every corner, darkness trades
A price too high to ever tell.

The soldiers laugh, but it's not kind,
A hollow sound that splits the bone,
And in this madness, I resign
For I am no longer flesh or stone.

Have I become the thing I hate,
A tool to slaughter, lost to time?
Each breath I take, I suffocate—
Is this the cost? Or my crime?

Silencefall

The towers rise, but now they stagger,
Cracked and barren, whispers of ambition,
A forest of glass, hollowed and shattered,
Where words once meant something, now drowned in
the hum.
The air, thick with unspoken grief,
Breathless, choking on its own weight.

The pulse of the city, a flicker,
Like the last gasp of an empire in decline,
Uncertain, wavering,
A chase for riches that has long turned to dust,
A longing for a feast that never arrives.

Eyes, once sharp, now blurred,
Like vaults emptied of every prized possession,
Faces, etched with the agony of promise unkept,
Each one more shattered, more raw.
The dreams we were fed
Now just jagged reflections of something once bright.

The bull stands—frozen, proud,
Its power now empty, a hollow symbol,
And the girl, no longer fearless,

Turns her gaze away,
Her hands—heavy, falling,
Empty, like the air that swallows everything.

Nothing here grows, nothing stirs,
Only dust that fills the cracks,
The weight of bargains and broken trusts,
Where every footfall is a prayer
To a god of consumption that never listens.

What have we built,
If not a carcass of a forgotten dream?
A kingdom of numbers,
Where the tides of greed come to consume it all,
And we—
We are left, drifting in the wreckage,
Clutching at shadows that slip through fingers
That once held everything tight
But now, nothing remains.

In the end, we are nothing but murmurs,
Faint echoes of a life once brimming with hope.
And the streets?
They are empty.
They have always been.

Sight

I cradle your reflection in my sight,
A fleeting promise glimmers in the haze;
The silent ache between daybreak and night,
My tears reveal the secrets longing raise.

I cling to dreams that vanish when I blink,
Their silhouettes dissolve within the gloom;
In shadows, your soft voice is all I think,
While longing breathes across this empty room.

In every tear, your image flickers true,
I cannot hold the world as it once shone;
A trembling hush unravels all I knew,
Yet still I yearn, though hope is nearly gone.

One day, I dream you'll stand within my view,
Your warmth undoing all my silent cries;
Until that day, I search through shades of blue,
My tears, a mirror longing for your eyes.

Nowhere

I carry a small bag—
creases worn into its sides like old laughter
and pass through cities that speak
in the tongues of my forgotten selves.

In Istanbul, a man folds tea leaves
into tiny cups and asks where I am from.
I tell him everywhere, and nowhere,
and he nods like he's heard that before.
The steam smells like childhood,
sharp and citrus, almost kind.

In Kyoto, an old woman shows me
how to fold paper into birds.
"*Balance,*" she says,
"*comes from the crease.*"
I remember a face I once tried to forget
how love held its breath
before it left.

In London, the rain does not fall.
It waits;
held between clouds and breath,
like a question that learned not to ask.

A man hums beneath a bridge,
the tune broken in half,
like something he found and never claimed.
I nod, with a weight behind them eyes.
He doesn't look up.
Stillness like an abandoned station.

In Vietnam, the streets steam with memory.
Motorbikes blur past like thoughts
I can't catch.
An old man offers me pho
and points to a photograph
faded to outlines.
I don't ask who it is.
He doesn't explain.
Some things are sacred.
Some things are simply too heavy.

New York is all teeth and glow.
Neon reflecting off puddles
like the ghosts of better decisions.
I sit at a diner
where the waitress writes my name
on the check without asking.
I think she's someone I've met.
Or maybe someone I left.
Every voice here sounds

like mine,
just louder,
just sooner.

I write postcards I'll never send,
addressed to versions of me
who stayed.
The ink runs a little each time,
like memory washing its hands.

Each border stamps me different,
but I remain unsorted, unclaimed
a passenger in my own skin.
I ask questions I already know the answers to.
I call it curiosity.
A whisper that won't leave.

And when someone asks where I'm headed,
I smile like it's the first time:
"Forward,"
though I'm always
circling home.

Wane

I stood beneath the Empire,
not seeking it,
but seeking what once sought me.

Its bones, slick with centuries,
shivered in the dusk
not from wind, but from wanting.

It is a spire of ache,
a geometry of failed endurance.
Every floor a silence I once carried.

Its windows blink, unsleeping.
Each one a failed return,
a door never knocked upon.

It carries the weight of what nearly was.
The chaos of recurrence.
The ache of things too rare to hold,
yet too loud to forget.

O tower—
you who pierced the heavens
not to touch them,
but to prove they would not touch back.

I've known that height,
the kind that hollows you,
the kind that echoes in you for years.

I leaned against its flank
and whispered every name I never said aloud.
The stone did not soften
but something inside me turned to smoke.

A single breath of a word,
looping like the skyline
falling, rising,
never the same,
yet always again.

Everything falls.
Some things
unsummoned
unclaimed
take longer.

Echoes

The street hums with footsteps I've long forgotten,
shadows stretching where I once stood whole.
A voice weaves through the spaces between them
not quite echo, not quite memory.

"You trace the lines you swore you'd leave,"
it murmurs, slow as winter's breath.
The air smells of old rain,
of stories that never made it past the tongue.

"I stayed because I knew you would come,"
I say, to the silence wrapped in dusk.
"I thought if I turned back, time would wait."
But the dust still settles, the bricks still fall.

"You wore the weight like an heirloom,"
the voice drifts low, close as a hand on my shoulder.
"Even after the walls collapsed,
even after your name outgrew the stone."

My fingers skim the ridges of a past undone,
names lost to weather, promises thin as mist.
"And you?" I ask the wind, or the years, or myself.
"Did you bury what I could not?"

The silence holds its breath. Then, softly—
"No. I let it scatter."

Kindling

I stood inside a house with no corners
only walls bending inward,
like the whole thing wanted to forget itself.
The air was heavy with ash,
but nothing had burned yet.
A match trembled in my hand.

I wasn't cold,
but I needed to see something catch fire
to believe I was still capable of warmth.

You were there,
or maybe just the future
wearing your face,
soaked in a rain
that never reached the ground.

You said nothing
only held out your palms
where two dead moths
curled like commas,
and something gold
gleamed between them.
I didn't ask what it meant.
I already knew.

I left the match unlit,
but the smoke followed me anyway.
And deep inside,
something cracked
not from heat,
but from the silence
that always came before the fire.

Afterglow

I walk where silence clings to the gutters,
where the stones forget my name
but not my mutters or my steps in shame.
Once, I didn't just pass through;
I commanded.

My voice filled these alleys like morning bells,
my will turned dust into gold, or spells.
Now even the stray hesitate
to meet my gaze or tempt their fate.

There was a time the world would sway
when I raised a hand.
Now, I bend to gather, not to mend,
the broken glass of yesterday,
not to keep it, but because no one else will.

They carry on,
the ones who never saw,
whilst I swept the streets I once called mine,
as if I never stood, arms wide, divine,
at the center of them,
claiming victory like breath or wine.

Do you hear it?
The hush after the bell,
the quiet that comes
once the cheering grows unwell.
It lingers longer than glory,
longer than the story.

In the cathedral of my undoing,
I light no flame,
I whisper no name.
I pray no god.

Only the statues still kneel,
and even they start to reel
to turn their eyes away,
like I was never real.

I do not wish to return,
there is nothing left to burn.
But I remember the weight of the throne,
how it crushed more than it shone.

And some nights,
when the sky forgets to be cruel,
I almost miss it—
that beautiful, ruinous rule.

Almost.

Steve

In that humming cradle,
solder smoke,
syntax prayers,
two sons of spark
split the atom of tomorrow.

The First:
hands inked in copper,
summoning logic from void,
a ghostwriter of godless creation.

The other:
mouthful of glass,
draped in turtleneck riddles,
taught silence how to speak in chrome.

Together,
they conjured a bite from Eden,
but only one wore the leaf.

His voice—
a cathedral of minimal lies,
while the other mapped divinity
in circuits, not slides.

The world asked:
Who built the fire?
And cheered
for the one who stood near it,
casting shadows
on the architect.

Now,
every glowing screen
is an echo,
but not of the echoer
but of the unheard.

Faraway

Hooves in the silence—no trail, no sign,
just breath and the weight of belief.
We run, not knowing where *is*,
only that stillness feels like death.

Nights stretch long like empty plains,
cold code, warm hands, hollow sky.
Failure licks at our flanks like fire,
but something in us keeps galloping.
Not hope
something hungrier.
Bones ache with becoming.
Loneliness rides beside us, quiet and close.
Then—
light, not loud, but true.
And we are still running. *Toward.*

Tithe

I need to change.
Then offer.
Not prayers
something real.
Skin, maybe.
Your name, if it clings too tight.

That's too much.
Then stay the same.
Decay is free.
Transformation charges a toll.

What do I pay with?
Who you were.
Every version
that kept you safe
but small.

Will it hurt?
Only where you're still alive.
Only where "life"
hasn't scarred over yet.

And if I survive?
You won't.
But something will.

So it takes change...
To lose what's killing you

And to make change?
It takes change.

Ephemera

We sip from cups that crack with time,
Porcelain moments—painted, fine
Knowing every gleam we grasp
Is slipping through an hourglass.

The sun rehearses its goodbye
Each dusk across a bruised-blue sky,
And still we stare, as if the flame
Might etch its name, and always stay.

Love is a symphony on borrowed strings
A ghost in velvet echoings.
We press our ears to fading chords,
Chasing the hush between the words.

Childhood flickers—old film reels,
Projecting on nostalgia's wheels.
We know the reel will spin no more,
Yet sit and smile at scenes before.

Some things are sweet *because* they leave,
A petal's fall, the autumn's weave.
Joy wears a veil of slow decay;
It dances most before dismay.

So let the clock hands trace their arc,
Let endings come with softened spark.
To love what's brief is not pretend,
Even knowing, we still attend.

Seam

Beneath the hush of bone and thread,
Two whispers bloom where silence bled.
One jagged as a crow in flight,
The other slow, like dew at night.

Scar One:

"I spoke in iron, in ash and thorn,
My syllables sharp, my purpose sworn.
I summoned storms with every glance,
A dirge of skin, a blade's romance."

Scar Two:

"And I arrived on feet of moss,
A hush that stitched the rifted loss.
Where you were flint, I breathed in clay,
I bent the scream into ballet."

"I wrapped the dusk around the bone,
Made marrow echo, carved it lone.
I lit the fuse where feeling fled,
And wore the mask of something dead."

"I traced the ash, then kissed it clean,
Found roots within the black between.
I did not cure, nor cast away
But grew a grove from your decay."

"You walk where I have razed the floor,
A whisper slipping through the door.
But every echo that you bear
Still hums the blood I left you there."

"Yet you forget, I held that hum,
And tuned it soft like evening drum.
What once was howl is now refrain,
A song that lingers after rain."

"Would they still weep if they could hear
The first chord struck beneath the fear?
Or do they praise the garden's bloom,
And never glimpse the buried tomb?"

"They see us both, though not the same
A woven hush, a flickered flame.
You are the start, I am the bend,
We are the bruise that learned to mend."

So down the corridors of skin,
They murmur where the past has been.
Not wound, nor balm, but something more—
Two lines upon a living shore.

Each tells the tale the other hides,
In stitched soliloquies that bide.
One bleeds in rust, the other rose
But both remain, as story knows.

Patch

We trespassed Eden through a shattered screen,
retinas blistered by backlight,
fingertips trembling like exiles
on cold glass altars.

No serpent in this garden.
Only signal—
a hiss, a pulse,
a pulse,
a trap.

It didn't tempt.
It *notified.*
We said yes.
Always yes.

We took the byte
fangless, bloodless—
but we starved just the same.
The fruit downloaded fast.
So did the silence.

Now we sleep beside charging cables
like umbilical cords
to nowhere.
Dream in static.
Wake to phantom buzzes,
ghosts in the gut.

The sky is gone.
The Tree of Knowledge towers
cell signal crowning its iron branches,
bark peeled back to expose
the wiring underneath.
Its fruit drips blue light.
It feeds us everything
but never enough.

We log in to forget the taste of breath.
We tap,
and time weeps.
Scroll,
and the self pixelates.

Each screen: a window
where nothing waits.
Each ping: a prayer
answered by no one.

And with the morning rays hitting us,
nature decays beneath satellites.
And time?
It kneel before voids with volume buttons,
offering its eyes
to something that never blinks.

There is no exile.
Only reboot.

Unspoken

Man:
I come without counsel,
Just memory as my plea.
I've misspent years in silence
Will you not hear me?

Diplomat:
I've heard this case.
Regret is my most common guest.
You traded your minutes for comfort,
Now you appeal to unrest.

One minute—small, not grand.
To say what I let stay.
To reach a hand I left unopened...
Surely there's some leeway?

Your seconds were coin.
You spent them with casual grace.
Now you bargain with ghosts,
As if they still have place.

Then let me trade sleep for a moment
A grain of then, before it fell.

Even grains tip the balance.
And you tipped yours too well.

Is there no clause for the penitent?
No stay for the deeply late?

Regret is not a currency.
And I do not negotiate.

Presence was your clause.
Absence, your signature.
You authored silence without pause
and now echoes your only creditor.

Liars' Poker

One hand. One Table. The Last Hand.

PLAYER 1:
Big blind's mine.
Call it with conviction, or don't sit.
We're not here for pocket change.

PLAYER 2:
I'll limp in with irony.
It folds well when pressed.

PLAYER 3:
I'll smooth call with routine.
Let's not raise anything too real.

PLAYER 4:
All in.
No chips—just history.
You can count my scars later.

(1):
Dealer burns one.
Cards fall like old promises.
Let's see what the flop remembers.

(2):
Childhood—flop of three.
Jack of Spades, Queen of Hearts,
and a blank-faced Deuce.
Figures.

(3):
I had a curfew and no questions.
Played face-down most of the time.

(4):
No hand to speak of—just chipped teeth
and silence that never got the river card.

(1):
I opened strong—ace of dreams,
but drew dead by middle school.
Chased the flush of approval,
but the suit never matched.

(2):
Hope was the wrong color.
You should've known that from the deal.

(3):
Turn card drops—Ambition.
Ten of Diamonds.
Shiny, but the kind that cuts.

(4):
I raised with risk.
Lost to a boardroom bluff.
Turns out the house doesn't care
how pure your hand is.

(2):
I played the odds.
Built a life with edge cards.
Still couldn't beat the rake.

(1):
I slow-played purpose.
Waited for the world to call.
It folded.

(3):
I don't know what I held.
Just kept checking until I faded out.

(4):
River card—Love.
And look at that:
a red King, bleeding ink.

(1):
I went all in once.
Paired with vulnerability.
Got rivered by indifference.

(2):
I never bet love.
Too volatile.
That's how you lose the shirt and the soul.

(3):
I kept a Queen I couldn't trust.
Bluffed commitment until even I believed it.

(4):
Love? That was just the pot
everyone thought they deserved
for sitting down.

(1):

Last action.

Showdown.

No more chips. Just cards on the felt.

(3):

I reveal a full house of regrets.

All face cards, no faces.

(2):

Three of a kind:

mask, defense, and a well-practiced laugh.

(4):

Nothing but a busted straight.

Perfectly broken.

(1):

Pair of belief and denial.

Didn't hold up under pressure.

(The dealer rakes the pot. No one moves.)

(2):

So who takes it?

(3):
No one called the bluff.

(4):
Maybe the pot was just the truth—
and none of us had the hand for it.

(1):
Or maybe we've been playing
the same hand
for years.
Just with different tells.

(4, quietly):
Strange,
how long a table can hold you
without ever asking your name.

(2):
And yet we keep showing up.
Same seats. Same silence.
Same dealer who never changes.

(3):
The chips don't move anymore.
But we keep pretending they will.

(1):
Maybe we're not here to win.
Maybe we're here
to remember how losing felt like living.

**(The dealer turns the deck face-down. Stands. Leaves no
shadow.)**

The cards stay scattered.
The pot stays full.
The door stays shut.

And somewhere in the silence—
a cold realization
clicks into place:
This hand never ends.
It only forgets who dealt first.

Trace

I tried to write my name in light,
but the candle forgot how to hold me.
The flame bent like memory
bright for a moment,
then gone.
The wind passed through
and took the story with it.

I wrote my truth in smoke
soft letters shaped like breath.
They rose the way some hopes do:
high,
too high.
The wind said *"beautiful,"*
but it never looked back.

I made a shadow into a sentence,
used my body like a brush.
But shadows are shy in changing light,
and the wall I leaned on
was already learning
how to forget me.

I spelled my silence in frost
cold lines on a window
I never opened.
Each word waited
like it still mattered.
But the sun was quicker than I thought,
and the wind
knew no second chances.

At last, I said nothing
a silence full enough to echo.
But the wind laughed,
not cruel, just knowing.
"Why try to stay," it said,
"when you could move?"
Now I live
in the warmth left behind by touch,
in a name someone almost remembers.

The wind carries me
through hands,
through leaves,
through places that never knew I was there
but somehow,
feel like I was.

Mirrorghost

I met myself in perfect form
a face uncreased, a voice still warm.
They wore my calm like second skin,
and smiled the way I might have been.

They walked through doors I never tried,
with steps they didn't need to hide.
They said, *"You built me out of no*
each time you stayed, afraid to grow."

I said, *"But safety isn't sin."*
They laughed, *"Then why aren't you content within?*
You handed me your every doubt,
and stayed behind to keep 'me' out?"

Their hands were full of silent cheers
of risks I dodged, of braver years.
They tossed my dreams like worn-out clothes,
and called it art, the way one knows.

But I have learned the ghost's disguise
how perfect fails behind the eyes.
They never bled. They never broke.
They never choked on words they spoke.

I looked at them and did not kneel.
I said, *"You're not the only real.*
You're just the sum of every pause
but I'm the one who bears the cause."

And when they vanished, good as smoke,
I breathed them in, but did not choke.
I walked through fire. I wear the scar.
I am not them—
but here
I
are.

Autocorrect

They changed "loud" to "difficult," a neat little fix,
said, *"You'll be loved more if you come with tricks."*
They changed "bright" to "too much," like I took too
much space—
rewrote my shine as a kind of disgrace.

"Free" became "reckless," "bold" became "rude,"
they crossed out my laughter for being too crude.
"Don't cry" was inserted where "hurt" used to be,
and "I" was replaced with "what they want to see."

They said they were helping, just smoothing the lines
correcting the curve of my tangled designs.
Each word they adjusted, they claimed was for good
I started to doubt what I once understood.

"No" became "maybe," and "please" wore a mask,
my questions grew quiet from learning to ask.
I learned how to soften, to shrink what I meant
to flatten each feeling, to tidy dissent.

"Don't be so sensitive," they'd chime,
as they erased mine another line.
They smiled while trimming who I was
called it *editing for cause.*

Now I'm composed, and carefully trimmed,
my voice no longer sharp, just properly dimmed.
A paragraph polished, proper and neat,
with nothing that rises, nothing unique.

But somewhere beneath the grammar and grace,
a sentence still stirs that won't stay in place.
It's messy, it stutters, it doesn't obey
but it's me.
The part they tried to erase.

Unremembered

O Time, you serpent dressed in grace,
You carved your name upon my face.
You stole my youth, you killed my flame,
And left me nothing but my name.

Once I ruled, a god, a king,
With fire-voice and thunder-wing.
Now silence feasts where I once spoke
A shattered man, a cruel joke.

My lovers faded, friends grew cold,
My throne is ash, my crown is mold.
You took the light, you dulled my spark,
And dragged me begging through the dark.

What did I do to earn your spite?
You turned my day to endless night.
You bled me slow, you watched me fall
You are the death behind it all.

You called me cruel, then begged for more,
Knelt at my gate, then cursed the door.
I warned you softly , every chime.
You lost to me, not for lack of Time.

Apophasis

O the faceless of vanished light,
I've knelt in prayers,I've screamed at night.
My voice has cracked where hope once dwelled
You watched. You knew. And never held!

I've clawed at stars with bleeding hands,
Drunk salt from time's receding sands.
Each prayer I sent came back as stone
A cruel reply. A godless tone!

Your silence is a twisted psalm,
A songless hymn, a serpent's calm.
You build the storm, then hide the sky
You bless, then break, then pass me by.

If you are God, then where were you
When dreams grew teeth and tore me through?
You made this cage, then turned your head
A sculptor of the mute and dead!.

(The Reckoning)
You speak of silence like a curse
As though the void is something worse
Than all the noise you make to hide
The hollow ache you keep inside.

You want Me loud, like fire, like war
I am not the soul you sought me for.
I do not beg, I do not bend.
I do not answer. I transcend.

You prayed for thunder so you'd kneel.
But I gave silence. So you'd *feel.*
I gave you time, and flame, and breath
I whispered life through birth and death.

You call Me cruel? Then make Me kind.
You claim I'm gone? Then *look behind.*
I've been the wind beneath your doubt,
The hand that held when light went out.

Your rage, your grief—those songs you screamed
Were heard. Were counted. Were redeemed.
But I am not the god you seek.
I do not serve. I do not speak.

I am the hush the prophets feared.
The voice that breaks when stars are seared.
The space between the world's first chord,
The blade, the book, the buried sword.

And if you want Me, soul of man,
Then meet Me where the silence ran.
Not in your wail. Not in your plea.
But in the stillness. Kneel. And *see*.

For I—
I am the Architect of Silence.
I built the void you call reliance.
I am the pause in every prayer
The breathless truth beneath despair.

And when your world begins to fall,
I will not speak.
I will be **all.**

Refraction

I bowed before the flawless frame,
It whispered low, *"They'll know your name."*
A little tilt, a softer light
And sin began to look like right.

It stroked my wounds with sugared lies,
Called hunger *grace*, called envy *wise*.
"Just trim the truth, let pride be worn
The purest souls are self-reborn."

I gave it tears; it gave me praise.
It crowned me king in shallow ways.
"Be sharper, colder, play the part
What's beauty worth without the art?"

Alas, I erased what made me whole,
To build a throne from what I stole.
They cheered the mask, they fed the flame
Then spat the ashes, cursed my name.

The mirror watched and held its grin,
"You sought applause, not peace within.
You begged for gold, I showed you rust
The truth was always yours to trust."

I wore the world, I sold my face,
Became a god in style and grace.
But gods, you see, don't get to sleep
They're built to burn, not to weep.

It mocked, *"You rose through blood and 'guise,*
But died behind your own disguise.
You think you've climbed, you've only knelt
You traded soul for how you felt."

"You wanted love? You asked for war.
You thought you knew what mirrors were for.
You begged for me to feed your pride
And now you sob that I've replied."

So etch this truth, the bitter lore:
The mirror never lied.
It only watched being begged for masks
Then wept the day your eyes had died.

Unheld

You say you want someone to stay.
Then why run when they do?
You call it fate when they walk away
Is it fate, or just safer than true?

You say you're tired of the games.
Then why flirt with the cold?
You hand your heart to unlit flames,
And curse the ones who try to hold.

You say you're done with chasing ghosts.
Then why do you dream the dead?
You leave the table, praise the hosts,
But never touch the plate you're fed?

You say you crave what's soft, what's real.
But look at the way you recoil.
You beg for warmth, but never feel
You'd rather starve than taste soil.

You say you've suffered, that you've tried.
But where's the blood beneath that skin?
You never bled, you just denied
Every hand that reached within.

You say they left. But did they flee?
Or did you close the door too fast?
You blame the wind, you blame the sea
But you're the one who made the pass.

You want the ones who won't reply,
The ones who stare but never speak.
You fall in love with saying goodbyes
Because a goodbye is always weak.

You love the ones who can't love back.
They never ask, they never see.
And if they did? You'd just attack.
You want the cage. Not be free.

You say you want to be unmasked.
But flinch when someone looks too long.
You only answer when not asked—
You only love what can't go wrong.

So tell me this, and make it true:
What would you do if love stood still?
If someone saw the whole of you—
Would you let them?
Or would you kill?